Black,
Universal,
Eternal

INSPIRATIONAL CHRISTIAN PROSE POETRY BY
RICKY CLEMONS

PUBLISHED BY FIDELI PUBLISHING, INC.

ISBN: 978-1-962402-17-0

Published by

Fideli Publishing, Inc.
119 W. Morgan St.
Martinsville, IN 46151

www.FideliPublishing.com

Table of Contents

Black, Universal, Eternal

The stars would not sparkle so bright and brilliant if the universe was not black and eternal, beyond this world, where black is what we make black to be around the clock.

The full, white moon would not glow so mystical if the night was not black, hovering over true, genuine lovers having no play act.

The ocean floors are deep and black for deep sea divers to explore, and almost every book is printed in black ink, which many more people will use instead of any other color of ink.

If black was evil, God would not have created the outer space so black and eternal.

Being black is not a bad thing to God, who made no mistake to create the universe black and fill it with galaxies of light year stars that are still not enough to fill up God's hand.

When we go to sleep, we will enter into a black, dark and peaceful quiet place where dreams will run so free without getting caught.

The black dark was upon the face of the deep before the spirit of God moved upon the face of the waters to show us that the color black has existed before the time on Earth for us to know when we read the first chapter of the book of Genesis.

The streetlights can shine so sophisticated in the black, dark night that gladly greets every race, creed and color of people so they can enjoy hanging out in the black, dark night.

God didn't make a mistake when He created black people, because black is so right with God, who appointed a black man to hold the highest office in this great nation.

Black is universal and eternal, beyond all the past, present and future generations here on Earth where black men, women, boys and girls are also God's creations.

God created the color black to fill the outer space, hovering over this world where everyone has a black and dark shadow that will waste no time to do what we do in the daylight and in the black, dark night with no complaints.

The color black is good and not evil, just like the heart can be so good or evil beneath the black, white, brown, red and yellow skin of rainbow colors wherever we go.

We so very often look at the color black as only being on Earth where black can be degraded below the black eternal universe.

Scientists and astronauts love to explore the unknown in the black, deep outer space that God created to surround His holy throne.

Many farmers will plow the black dirt on the ground and plant seeds to grow grass, trees, flowers and plants all around the world.

Almost everyone has a TV in their home and every TV has a black screen.

When the TV is off and quiet, we pass by it without getting disturbed.

A lot of businessmen love to wear black suits.

Many church choir members and clergymen will wear black robes.

Many dancers in the nightclubs will reach up to the highest peak of their fantasy in the dark nightclubs, swirling around psychedelic lights that pierce through the black dark appearance of attracting romance.

God created the universe black and eternal.

Only here on earth human beings can be opinionated about the color of the skin in every land.

An auditorium must be dark for the stage lights to illuminate the performers so they can captivate the audience, who won't fake their reactions in the dark auditorium.

A movie theater must be dark for the characters to look like they can grab you and me and pull us into the big screen so fast.

Black is a very positive color.

We can get a good night's sleep in the dark that is very black.

Soldiers are also trained to fight in the black dark night to be their advantage to win the war because of their eyes being adjusted to good night vision.

Black is universal and eternal in the outer space where white is universal and eternal; both have something in common beyond the race of every human being who God wonderfully made with the color that He chose to color our faces that we should like when we look in the mirror.

Regardless of what others see, God believes that He made no mistake having given you and me the color of our skin.

Black is universal and eternal in the outerspace while here on earth the black skin has been degraded to be less than an ape to get more honor especially from evolutionists believing that we black people evolved from apes.

The black holes in the universe are so powerful to suck up billions of massive stars to lose their brilliant light shining brighter than a thousand suns.

Black was originated by God who created the black holes to serve His purpose in the vast universe.

God also created us black people with a much better purpose to blend in with every other race of Christian people to complete God's replacement of the fallen angels from heaven where also we black Christians will be eternal beyond maybe billions of universes and other worlds.

We Are Not Going Anywhere

We black people are not going anywhere when we also have made this nation great.

Today, we black people not only belong here in America, we belong here in this whole world that God created us to live in with every other race, creed and culture of people.

Our black lives matter to God, who created us to be distinct from every other race of people.

Our black distinction is of very good use to God every day that we are not going anywhere away from this world.

The world is also our world for us black people to enjoy living in, and prejudice and oppression can't take our joy away.

We are like the oceans that will not go anywhere.

We are like the sky that will not go anywhere.

We are like the ground that will not go anywhere.

We are like the universe that will not go anywhere.

We black people are here to stay until Jesus Christ comes back again to also take many of us black people back to heaven with Him.

Time has always been on our side to help us black people immigrate all over this world.

Time was on our ancestors' side to help them claim their presence for being here in this world.

Most of all, God has always been on our side to bring us black people this far for us to know that we are not going anywhere from making good contributions to this world.

Many of us black people contribute our talents and skills to this world.

Many of us black people contribute our time and peace to this world.

Many of us black people contribute our love and intelligence to this world.

Many of us black people contribute our education and faith in God to this world.

We black people are not going anywhere when many of us black people are hard-working people and getting less pay.

Many of us black people have a fear for God.

We black people are not going anywhere away from this world.

We are like the air that will not go away.

This world will one day come to an end and go down into fire and brimstone, when many of us black people will also be in the new Jerusalem Holy City with Jesus Christ and every other race of people who are saved in Jesus Christ.

All of us saved black people will not go anywhere away from the new heaven and new earth that Jesus will create for all of the saints.

We black people are not going anywhere in a world of injustice toward us.

We black people are not going anywhere in a world of inequality toward us. We are not going anywhere in a world of prejudice toward us.

We are not going anywhere in a world of oppression toward us.

We are not going anywhere in a world of discrimination toward us.

We are not going anywhere in a world of hatred toward us.

We black people were destined by God to live in this world.

Many of us black people are not going anywhere away from putting in our efforts to make this world a better place for everybody to live in.

Many of us black people are not going anywhere away from loving our neighbors in every race, creed and culture of people.

We black people are here to stay in this world for as long as we exist.

The sand will run out of an hourglass, but we black people are not going anywhere away from this world.

Water will run down a drain, but we black people are not going anywhere away from this world.

A tornado will blow a house down, but we black people are not going anywhere away from this world.

Prejudice will not cause us to go anywhere away from this world.

Injustice will not cause us to go anywhere away from this world.

Discrimination will not cause us to go anywhere away from this world.

Inequality will not cause us to go anywhere away from this world.

Hatred will not cause us to go anywhere away from this world.

Oppression will not cause us to go anywhere away from this world.

Stereotyping will not cause us to go anywhere away from this world.

God created us black people to live in this world with every other race of people.

We black people are not going anywhere away from this world that has plenty of space for us black people to live in.

We black people are not going anywhere away from ignorance.

The sun will rise and set on us black people.

The sun will not move anywhere away from us all day long.

The moonlight will glow down on us black people.

The moonlight will not move anywhere away from us all night long.

The stars will sparkle down on us black people.

The stars will not move anywhere away from us all night long.

Nature doesn't want us black people to go anywhere away from this world.

Many racist people will move far away from us black people, if they don't want to live next to us black people.

Many of us black people still love them, but we will not accept their prejudices against us.

If the sun stops shining, we are not going anywhere away from this world.

If the moonlight stops glowing, we are not going anywhere away from this world.

If the stars stop sparkling, we are not going anywhere away from this world.

If the rivers stop running into the oceans, we are not going anywhere away from this world.

If all the harvested crops dry up, we are not going anywhere away from this world.

Evolution can spread like the Corona virus, but we black people are not going anywhere away from this world.

This world is also our world to live in until Jesus Christ comes back again.

This great nation is also our nation to live in until Jesus Christ comes back again.

Many of us black people love the color of our skin.

If some black people don't like the way they look, then they don't like the way that God created them to look.

God didn't make any mistakes when He created us black people.

Racist people believe that we black people weren't created in the image of God.

God hates prejudice, whether its many white people being prejudiced against black people or whether it's many black people being prejudiced against white people.

There is nothing good about being prejudiced against anyone.

We black people will always exist and will not go anywhere away from this world of many prejudiced people who can't get rid of us black people, because God won't allow them to succeed in doing that.

If Being Black is a Crime

If being black is a crime then God, Himself, committed a crime for creating black men, women, boys and girls.

Many people believe that all black people are criminals living among them day after day.

How can it be a crime to be black when God has blessed many black people to get a good education?

How can it be a crime to be black when God has blessed many black people to be great athletes?

How can it be a crime to be black when we had a black president?

How can it be a crime to be black when there is a black woman vice president?

How can it be a crime to be black when there are black judges?

How can it be a crime to be black when there are black doctors?

How can it be a crime to be black when there are black surgeons?

God didn't commit a crime when He created a black man like me.

How can it be a crime to be black when there are black scientists?

How can it be a crime to be black when there are black mayors?

How can it be a crime to be black when there are black movie stars?

How can it be a crime to be black when there are black police officers and chiefs of police?

How can it be a crime to be black when there are black gymnasts?

No one can accuse God of committing a crime for creating black men, women, boys and girls in His image.

No one can arrest God for creating black people.

No one can handcuff God for creating black people.

No one can shoot God for creating black people.

No one can put a chokehold on God for creating black people.

No one can lock God up in jail for creating black people.

No one can give God a lifetime sentence for creating black people.

So how can it be a crime to be black when there are black preachers?

How can it be a crime to be black when there are black school teachers?

How can it be a crime to be black when there are black nurses?

How can it be a crime to be black when there are black college professors?

How can it be a crime to be black when there are black ballet dancers?

How can it be a crime to be black when there are black mechanics?

How can it be a crime to be black when there are black social workers?

How can it be a crime to be black when there are black engineers?

How can it be a crime to be black when there are black millionaires and billionaires?

If being black is a crime, then God would only allow black murderers to get the death penalty.

God, Himself, will make sure that white people see His wrath upon only black murderers.

How can it be a crime to be black when there are black soldiers who fought in wars so that we can live our lives in freedom?

How can it be a crime to be black when there are black senators speaking out for equality and justice for all people in this great nation?

How can it be a crime to be black when there are black news journalists?

How can it be a crime to be black when there are black chefs who can cook some of the best meals in this world?

How can it be a crime to be black when many black people are the best employers on their jobs?

God created wonderfully made black people, just like He did every other race of people.

If being black is a crime, then God would only judge black people, but that's so not true of what God would do.

If being black is a crime God would not even allow a dog to live with black people.

If being black is a crime, then God wouldn't allow a white man or white woman to go to prison for committing a crime.

How can it be a crime to be black when there are black artists?

If being black is a crime, then God would be an unjust God.

If being black is a crime, then God would sentence every black man, woman, boy and girl to burn in hell.

If being black is a crime, then Jesus would have left black people out of His saving grace.

Jesus would not have died for the sins of black people.

If being black is a crime, then Jesus will not take any black person to heaven with Him when He comes back again.

If being black is a crime, then why would black people even exist?

God created black people to exist in this old world.

How can it be a crime to be black when there are black military officers?

How can it be a crime to be black when there are black real estate agents?

How can it be a crime to be black when there are black-owned businesses?

How can it be a crime to be black when there are black aircraft pilots?

How can it be a crime to be black when there are black Christians?

If being black is a crime, then God would only allow black people to be locked up in prison.

Being black is no crime to God, even though it seems that being black is a crime to many people of another race.

They might look at being black as a threat to them, and they won't trust anyone who is black.

If being black is a crime, then God would had never created black people to live in this world.

If being black is a crime, then God owes it to every black man, woman, boy and girl to tell us why we are criminals.

If being black is a crime, then all of us black people would be criminals in God's eyesight.

If being black is a crime, then God would allow the ignorance of other races of people to be the right thing to judge black people every day.

Being black is no crime to God, who can heal our wounds of inequality, segregation, discrimination, injustice and oppression that's been going on for hundreds of years.

One day soon, Jesus Christ will come back again and put an end to all of this racism and racists will burn in hell.

Racism is a criminal to God every day.

How can it be a crime to be black when there are black firefighters?

How can it be a crime to be black when there are black carpenters?

Being black is no crime to God, but being black is a crime to anyone who is prejudiced against black people.

God didn't commit a crime when He created black people to live in this world.

We black people are under the microscope of injustice that makes all of us look like we were born in this world to be only criminals.

If being black is a crime, then God would not have allowed black people to integrate with other cultures of people.

Being black is no crime to God, who doesn't love any other race of people more than He loves us black people.

The Dream is Alive

Dr. Martin Luther King Jr.'s dream is alive and living in black people working a legal job to give them the drive to reach high and excel to their full potential.

That keeps the dream alive and well in many black people looking good, and far from not having a dollar in their pocket.

The dream is living in good black doctors, nurses, firefighters and police officers making the dream to be a proven fact.

It's living in good black school teachers and students leading the states and nation to keep the dream living.

It's living in good black political leaders being hard to replace.

It's living in black entertainers and talk show hosts popular today from coast to coast.

It's living where ambitious and courageous black people are going to college near and far from home, where black college students can get in their cars and drive back and forth to college every day.

It's living in many good black military people who are brilliant military officers, and are not a rare thing in the military today, where good black Navy Seals, Marines and Army soldiers are some of the best fighters on the front lines.

We keep the dream living in good black people who express their freedom of speech and religion.

It's living in many black Christian people who make the right decision every day — to love Jesus Christ and their good and bad black and white neighbors.

Dr. King's dream is alive, despite the black-on-black crimes that have no power to kill the dream.

The dream packs a good lunch for black people who have a big appetite for knowledge and success, which every black American can take a big bite of and swallow down to keep the dream living in young black children who are smart and so innocent.

The dream gives every black man, woman, boy and girl the opportunity to change the world and make it a better place to live, which won't happen if negative black people believe the dream cannot take them to the mountaintops that Dr. Martin Luther King Jr. saw.

The dream lives on in especially we Christian Black people who love to give Jesus Christ all the glory and praise that Dr. King did when he lived with his great dream that woke up this world out of its spiritual unconciousness to see that all human beings are created in the image of God.

If Dr. King was Alive Today

If Dr. Martin Luther King Jr. was alive today, what would he say especially to many black women and black men making babies out of wedlock?

If Dr. Martin Luther King Jr. was alive today, what would he say especially to many black men being locked up in prison?

If Dr. Martin Luther King Jr. was alive today, what would he say especially about black-on-black crimes?

Dr. King didn't believe in violence against anyone, whether they were black, white, brown, yellow or red.

If Dr. Martin Luther King Jr. was alive today, what would he say especially to black couples divorcing one another?

Dr. King was a God-fearing man.

He would have understood if there were some unfaithfulness or some abandonment or abuse going on in the marriage.

If Dr. Martin Luther King Jr. was alive today, he would feel so good about black people loving the Lord and being good to everybody.

If Dr. Martin Luther King Jr. was alive today, what would he say to many black people not pulling together?

If Dr. Martin Luther King Jr. was alive today, what would he say to black men and black women selling drugs, especially to their own black people?

If Dr. Martin Luther King Jr. was alive today, what would he say about many black churches that worship money, accomplishments and material things?

If Dr. Martin Luther King Jr. was alive today, he would feel so good about Barack Obama being the first black president of the United States of America.

He would know that his dream is extraordinary.

If Dr. Martin Luther King Jr. was alive today, he would be speaking out against police violence towards black men.

If Dr. Martin Luther King Jr. was alive today, he would speak peace in other countries.

If Dr. Martin Luther King Jr. was alive today, he would give some wise advice to President Donald Trump and his staff.

If Dr. Martin Luther King Jr. was alive today, he would feel so good about black men, women, boys and girls getting a good education.

If Dr. Martin Luther King Jr. was alive today, what would he say about many black men abusing black women and not taking care of their children?

If Dr. Martin Luther King Jr. was alive today, what would he say about many black children cursing out their single mothers?

If Dr. Martin Luther King Jr. was alive today, he would feel so good about many young black people going to college and getting their degrees.

If Dr. Martin Luther King Jr. was alive today, what would he say about many black men and women using drugs?

If Dr. Martin Luther King Jr. was alive today, what would he especially say about black gangs killing many of their own black people?

I believe that if Dr. Martin Luther King JR. was alive today, he would encourage people in every race to treat everybody right.

He would visit every state to speak words of wisdom, love, peace and justice to make this nation stand out before other nations.

Dr. Martin Luther King Jr. would inspire people to be the best they can be in this life that is short.

He would encourage especially black men and black women to not hold grudges against white people who had many ancestors who enslaved black people for worldly gain.

If Dr. Martin Luther King Jr. was alive today, he would love and respect everybody and encourage everybody to do God's holy will.

He would not speak words to divide the nation.

Dr. Martin Luther King Jr. would give some good advice, especially to black people to humble themselves before the Lord as they prosper in life.

I believe that Dr. Martin Luther King Jr. would inspire the political leaders to be trustworthy and honest before the people of the nation.

If Dr. Martin Luther King Jr. was alive today, I believe he would know that there is still a lot of work to be done, especially for black men to not be an endangered species to the white society.

Dr. Martin Luther King Jr.'s dream was from the Lord.

His dream is every black American's reality today.

When Dr. Martin Luther King Jr. was alive, he worshipped God who gave him the courage and intelligence to speak out on equality.

The Color of the Skin

Many human beings will see the color of the skin to be a problem day after day.

Little babies don't see color when someone holds them, and a dog doesn't see color when someone plays with it or pulls its tail.

Many human beings can be hung up on color, but the sun sees no color when it shines down on you and me.

The air doesn't care about what color our skin is as we breathe it in and out of our nostrils so we can live our lives.

The seasons see no color of the skin and won't leave us out of its seasons because of our skin color.

Many human beings don't like the color of their skin and will try to change the color that God gave to them to be right by Him.

The ground has no problem with the color of our skin and holds us all up every day and every night, even though many human beings are like an earthquake to shake down the color of the skin to rubble.

Nature sees no color of the skin as it gives you and me its tranquility, but the sinful nature of many human beings makes them see the color of the skin like a natural disaster.

No one can say to God, "You were wrong for giving me the color that I am," because God cannot lie about the way that He made you and me to look.

God has no problem with the color of the skin, but many people are hooked on a certain color.

No matter what the color of the skin is, sickness and death don't care about who we are that sin will be so unfair to.

God is fair to every human being who He loves all the same, but many human beings will pick and choose who to love according to the color of the skin.

Many human beings don't like every color that God created for His pleasure, but it's God who colored who He wanted to color apart from what we like and don't like.

God's holy law shows no respect for whoever breaks it and sins against God who sees no color of skin to be guilty before Him in the presence of His angels.

There is no end to color in God, who gives us different colors of the skin that many human beings will degrade for their own selfish reasons, which is so deranged.

Hating people for the color of their skin is a very strange thing to God, who gives us all a life to live no matter the color of our skin.

The righteous will go to heaven, regardless of the color of the skin.

Hell has no barrier to all who rebel against God who no human being has ever seen, except Jesus Christ, His only begotten Son.

God had given His Son the right skin color and He was still hated by many human beings from sun up to sun down.

Many people of His color hated Him for who He was and still is — the Son of God.

There is no color barrier in love, because love sees no color; only prejudice sees color.

Many human beings are prejudiced, no matter the color of the skin under all the stars.

There is nothing wrong about color, but many human beings will make the color of the skin to be wrong and a big mistake.

What's worse is to dislike one's own skin color because of someone else's opinion of you.

God didn't make a mistake when He made you different from someone else.

Love your color that God gave you for yourself.

Look in the mirror and see that you are wonderfully made by God.

Animals don't care about what color we are, but many human beings will care as if God didn't know what He was doing when he created people of color.

The color of the skin shouldn't matter to any of us.

The difference is all in people's minds.

What we think will flow from our lips that God gave us to speak good words about people, no matter the color of the skin.

From the beginning of this world all the way down to the end of this world, every human being's blood is red.

If we need some blood to keep on living, we won't care who we get it from because life is more important than the color of the skin, and many human beings will admit to this.

How can we find fault in God, who created every human being to give Him our time and love?

God has no faults, but human beings have many especially when they are opinionating about the color of the skin.

Beauty is in the eye of the beholder, but color is in the eye of the judgmental human being who will make color to be a problem under the sky.

The Black Voice

The black voice has been speaking out for four hundred years.

That black voice spoke words of bondage with pleas to be set free from slavery.

The white slave owners ignored the black voice for 400 years, but the black voice couldn't keep silent.

The black voice talked about being in chains and shackles down in the old wooden ships that made their way across the ocean waters with very little medical treatment and only a little food to eat.

The black voice talked about being whipped many times for not having enough energy to row the ships so they could reach the sandy beaches on time to meet the new slave owners.

The white slave owners were eager to not hear the black voice telling them that what they were doing was not right.

The white slave owners just didn't want to listen to the black voice that was frightened and vulnerable in the new land where the black voice ended up.

The black voice was purchased by the slave traders in the new land.

The black voice made a loud cry of anguish, disappointment and heartache for the white slave owners to hear, but they just didn't care about setting the black voice free from their white voices enslaving them.

The black voice was told to be quiet and suck it up.

The black voice was wise to not say too much and to not get too tired and weary.

The black voice hummed and sang spiritual songs of freedom in the hot cotton fields where God also heard the black voices sounding so joyful.

The black voice asked God to set them free from slavery one day.

On the quiet nights, the black voice would sound strong in prayer before laying down to sleep.

The black voice would also hear God's voice in their dreams of freedom.

The black voice whispered words of hope in the Underground Railroad as they tried to flee the South and get to the North.

God gave the black voice the power to speak up and speak out against slavery.

God gave the black voice the wisdom to speak out against inequality.

God gave the black voice the knowledge to speak out against segregation.

God gave the black voice the courage to speak out against discrimination.

God gave the black voice the motivation to speak out against injustice.

God gave the black voice the strength to speak out against police brutality.

God fully supported the black voice as it spoke out in love.

God fully supported the black voice when it spoke out in peace.

God fully supported the black voice when it spoke out in joy.

God fully supported the black voice when it spoke out in courage.

God fully supported the black voice when it spoke out in contentment.

God is for the black voice and not against the black voice.

God wanted the black voice to speak up and speak out against prejudice.

God empowered the black voice for thousands of years, going all the way back to Zipporah, the wife of Moses, who Miriam didn't accept because Zipporah wasn't a Hebrew.

God empowered Zipporah to be a strong black woman who didn't let Miriam get her down.

The black voice is still strong today in the news media.

The black voice is still strong today in the church.

The black voice is still strong today in the military.

The black voice is still strong today in protest.

The black voice is still strong today in entertainment.

The black voice is still strong today in sports.

The black voice is still strong today in the home.

The black voice is still strong today in this great nation that the black voice helped to make great.

The black voice is still strong today in the medical field.

The black voice is still strong today in the government.

The black voice is still strong today in science.

The black voice is still strong today in technology.

The black voice is still strong today in the Olympics.

The black voice is still strong today all around the world.

Regardless of the bruises that the black voice got, it couldn't keep the black voice from being heard by God.

Regardless of the sores that the black voice got, it couldn't keep the black voice from being respected by God.

Regardless of the pain that the black voice experienced, it couldn't keep the black voice from being in favor with God.

Regardless of how sick the black voice became, it couldn't keep the black voice from being healed by God.

Regardless of the flaws the black voice had, it never kept the black voice from being blessed by God.

The black voice is a threat to prejudiced people, and the black voice is like a fruit tree to God.

The black voice is a curse to prejudiced people, but the black voice is like good health to God.

The black voice is an enemy to prejudiced people, but the black voice is a friend to God.

The black voice is like a little canoe to prejudiced people, but the black voice is like an aircraft carrier ship to God.

The black voice is the voice of yesterday, today and tomorrow, when the black voice will not keep silent against inhumanity, which is something God will never support.

God greatly supports the black voice.

The Black Dream

The black dream is for oppression to end upon black people.

The black dream is for equal opportunity to come alive for all black people.

The black dream is for justice for all black people.

The black dream is for no economic slavery upon black people.

The black dream is for all black people to have the privilege to buy a house.

The black dream is for black people to be treated right by all people of another race.

The black dream is for all black people to prosper.

The black dream is for all black people to not be looked down upon.

The black dream is for all black people to forgive white people.

The black dream is for all black people to love ourselves, regardless of what prejudiced people say or do.

The black dream is for all black people to love being black.

The black dream is for all black people to treat everybody right.

The black dream is for all black people to come out of the wilderness of inequality.

The black dream is for all black people to come out of their dark cave of silence and not let violence and brutality upon black people keep going on.

The black dream is for all black people to turn back to God.

The black dream is for all black people to know that they are somebody who can choose to do good things in this world.

The black dream is for all black people to move on beyond prejudiced people.

The black dream is for all black people to know the past dark days of 400 years of slavery are over and use that knowledge to work for justice and liberty today.

The black dream is for all black people to show prejudiced people that we are not like them who love to hate black people and brown people.

The black dream is a very powerful dream that will greatly disturb prejudiced people who can't kill the black dream.

The black dream is very real in many black people who will protect it to get justice.

The black dream is very real in many black people who are bold and stand up for change.

The black dream is very real in many black people who live their lives for civil rights.

The black dream is very real in many black people who won't let black history die and be forgotten like there was no 400 years of black slavery in this nation.

The black dream is very real in many black Christians who love and forgive their prejudiced enemies.

The black dream is like the full, white moonlight shining all night long.

The black dream is like a beautiful rainbow arching across the sky after the rain.

The black dream is like the sunlight melting the snow after a snow blizzard is over.

The black dream is like the beautiful flowers that bloom in the springtime.

The black dream is like clean water running from the spring.

The black dream is for all black people to be healed from prejudice.

The black dream is for all black people to come together to make this world a better place to live in.

The black dream is for all black people to dream with our eyes open wide and see that we are making a difference in educating this nation so others are not ignorant about who we are.

The black dream is for all black people to dream big so that we can be understood by other races of people so they won't judge us all to be criminals.

The black dream is for all black people to dream with their eyes opened wide to see that true freedom is loving God and keeping His Commandments.

The black dream is for all great and small black people to look deep within themselves and let Jesus Christ in to help them to not be prejudiced against another race of people or our own black people.

Many of our own black people are prejudiced against one another.

Some dark-skinned black people don't like light-skinned black people.

Some light-skinned black people don't like dark-skinned black people.

Many of the brown-skinned black people are caught in the middle.

The black dream is a great dream that all black people can hold onto for as long as we live.

Prejudiced people can't take away our black dream.

Our black dream is very real to us every day.

Our black dream is a dream that God gave to all of us black people.

The black dream is for all of us black people to dream with our eyes opened wide so we can see that God didn't bring us this far to let us down and allow the past to repeat itself.

God gave us a great dream that prejudiced people don't respect and will mock.

God has shined His sunlight on our black dream and our black existence all around the world.

Our black dream is a dream that we black people can see with our eyes open wide so our black dream can be real and active in our black lives.

When we lay down to sleep, we will have some dreams until we wake up and those dreams fade away, but our black dream will never fade away because it is very real in our daily living.

Our black dream began with our black ancestors, who never gave up their black dream and passed it down to us black people today.

Our black ancestors had a dream of a better day for you and me, and we need to make sure that dream was not in vain.

The black dream is the vision of the past, present and future for all of us black people who put God first in our lives and give Him the glory and praise for our black dream.

The Black Will

The black will penetrated through the iron wall of 400 years of slavery.

The black will is strong, like hurricane winds.

The black will has blown down many years of segregation.

The black will is like a high mountain cliff where people stand on the edge and do not fall off into hopelessness.

The black will is like a light at the end of the dark tunnel of inequality.

The black will is like the deep oceans.

The black will is deep in perseverance.

The black will is like a peaceful river that flows.

The black church has flowed peacefully in this troubled nation.

The black will is like a sunny, warm day.

The black will shines its warmth through the police violence and brutality on black people.

The black will is like the full, white moon shining so mysterious all night long.

The black will shines so mysterious with endurance so other races of people can see that we black people are survivors in this world.

The black will is like all the stars sparkling in the night.

Our black ancestors birthed our black people to be here today so we can sparkle in the night of injustice.

The black will is like a fruit tree planted near the water.

Through the many years in this nation, we black people have grown many fruits of talents, skills, wisdom and knowledge to help make this nation great today.

The black will is like the deep valleys that run between the hills and mountains.

We black people are down in the deep valleys of not getting all the privileges that this nation only gives to those who are favored to be privileged.

The black will is like a cruise ship on the ocean waters.

Our black ancestors cruised through the rugged waves of 400 years of slavery so us black people could enjoy our freedom today.

The black will is like the rooster that crowed at Peter for denying Jesus Christ three times.

The black will crows at prejudiced people who deny Jesus and hate people, no matter what their skin color is.

God's will gave birth to the black will and let it grow up strong over 400 years of slavery.

The black will found favor with God for us black people to not ever be extinct in this world.

The black will is like the Grand Canyon that is very massive.

We black people are very massive in numbers all around the world.

The black will is like a published book.

Our black lives are like a book for all the world to read and see that our black lives are a best-seller.

The black will has been through rugged terrain and disappointment.

The black will has been through the wilderness of heartaches.
The black will has been through the tidal waves of being misunderstood.

The black will has been through the earthquakes of hardships.

The black will today is going through the heatwaves of being treated unfairly.

The black will today is going through the snow blizzards of being disrespected.

The black will today is going through the polluted waters of violence.

The black will today is breathing in and out the polluted air of people who are not concerned about what's going on with us black people.

The black will is a great thing for all of us black people to always hold onto because the black will is the choices that every black man, woman, boy and girl can make for being mature in one's right mind.

Our black ancestors made their choices in their black will that God gave to them.

They chose to keep on living the best way that they could through years of slavery.

The black will has also affected many prejudiced people and made them feel guilty about treating black people badly.

The black will is very popular with the angels in heaven, but the black will is not popular with prejudiced people.

Work on Being Black

Work on being black and don't try to be white, because white people don't truly know what it's like to be black.

Work on being black because being a black man, woman, boy and girl is who you are.

God accepted you and me for being black, so who are we to not accept ourselves for being black?

If you work on being black, it will be a joy to be who God created you and me to be.

Working on being black will bring out more of our talents.

Working on being black will bring out more of our honesty

Working on being black will bring out more of our awareness.

Working on being black will bring out more of our presence.

Working on being black will bring out more of our love for ourselves and other races of people.

Many black people work on being accepted by other races of people.

Other races of people are more willing to accept us black people if we love the way that God created us to be.

Work on being black because many of us black people are very intelligent.

Work on being black because many of us black people are very spiritual people.

Work on being black because many of us black people are good people.

Work on being black because many of us black people are very wise people.

Work on being black because many of us black people are loving people.

Work on being black because many of us black people are respectful people.

Work on being black because many of us black people are very successful people.

Work on being black because many of us black people are creative people.

Work on being black because many of us black people are God-fearing people.

Other races of people are more willing to respect us black people if they see that we respect ourselves.

Other races of people are more willing to love us black people if they see that we black people love ourselves and love them.

Other races of people are more willing to help us black people if they see that we will help ourselves.

Other races of people are more willing to not judge us black people if they see that we accept ourselves for who we are.

Work on being black because being black is a great treasure to God.

Work on being black because being black brings forth good fruits from the black dirt in the ground.

Work on being black because being black is like a quiet dark night where we can get a good night's sleep.

Work on being black because being black is like the bold black universe that is forever present.

Work on being black because being black is beautiful upon many black women.

Work on being black because working on being black is not committing a crime that is also committed by other races of people.

Working on being black is freedom from deceiving ourselves that we are white when we are really black.

Work on being black because black will be around forever.

Many black people will work hard on their jobs, but they won't work on being black.

Many black people will work hard on their marriages, but they won't work on being black.

Many black people will work hard on their education, but they won't work on being black.

Many black people will work hard in the church, but they won't work on being black.

The Lord Jesus Christ wants you and me to work on being black because He created us to be black.

Work on being black because it's our purpose in life to be black and love and obey the Lord Jesus Christ.

Many black people don't love being black because they were told that black is ugly.

Many black people don't love being black because they were told that black is inferior.

Many black people don't love being black because they were told that black is dumb.

Many black people don't love being black because they were told that black is evil.

Work on being black because it is not a sin to be black.

Work on being black because black is strong to withstand prejudice and discrimination.

Work on being black because black is encouraged to take on oppression and injustice.

Work on being black because black is here to stay through the storms of police brutality upon black people.

Work on being black because black is shade from the hot, scorching sunlight of inequality.

Work on being black that is a champion over not being held back from achieving greatness.

Work on being black that is a warrior defeating stereotyping.

Work on being black that God cheerfully colored with His eternal crayon that no other race of people can break or throw away.

Work on being black like the sun works on shining its bright light down on us all day long.

Work on being black all day long to shine our black existence in this dark world.

Work on being black because Jesus Christ has worked out our soul's salvation for us black people to be saved.

Many people will degrade us for being black, but we can work on being black for God so He can work His unique presence into our black lives.

Work on being black because being black is not giving up on setting our minds to accomplishing our dreams.

Working on being black is facing up to many ignorant people of other races.

Many of our black men will work on killing one another and not work on being black and loving one another.

Many of our black people will work on pulling one another down like crabs in a barrel and not work on being black and pulling together.

Work on being black because God created us black people for His holy purpose.

Working on being black is a waste of time to black people who don't respect themselves.

Working on being black is a joke to black people who mistreat their own black people.

Work on being black because being black is trusting the Lord who many of our ancestors trusted through their hardships.

Work on being black because being black is real proof of survival in this world.

Work on being black because being black is greatly approved by God, who created us to live among other races of people every day.

We Black Human Beings

We black human beings were created in the image of God, who also loves us black human beings.

Many of us black human beings love our light skin, light brown skin, medium brown skin, dark brown skin and dark skin complexions.

We black human beings are profound souls with a strong will to live and survive against injustice and prejudice.

Our black ancestors are the crowns on the heads of our black history that sings joyful and victorious songs about us still existing today.

God smiled down from heaven and said, "I will create black human beings to populate the Earth with black men, women, boys and girls."

We black human beings are like the ocean waves splashing against the hard rocks of injustice, prejudice and discrimination that we black human beings face every day.

We black human beings are like beautiful furniture in the house of this world, where the dust of hatred against us covers over us every day.

We black human beings are like the seasons that change — we go through the changes of not knowing when the policemen will come our way to shoot us down when many of us are innocent.

We black human beings are like the full white moonlight's glow — we glow our gifts, talents and skills all through the dark nights of oppression.

We black human beings are like a beautiful pathway that other races of people can walk down and see how our black ancestors prosper in this great nation.

We black human beings are like the beautiful rainbow in the sky so that people of other races can see that we black human beings have different complexions and like a rainbow of people up in the sky of life.

We black human beings are the soul music to melt people's hearts to change for the better to bring love, peace, unity and equality.

We black human beings are beautiful to God, who wonderfully made us.

As long as we are beautiful to God, it doesn't matter what people of other races think of us day after day.

The sunlight treats us black human beings right every day.

The moonlight treats us black human beings right every night.

The great blue sky treats us black human beings right every day and every night.

Nature treats us black human beings right all of the time.

We black human beings are like a deep mystery to many people of other races, and many of them can't solve our black presence in this world because many of them were taught that we black human beings evolved from apes.

Our black ancestors are like a bridge that every black man, woman, boy and girl can cross over to get to the opportunity of an education.

We black human beings are like a good movie, and can move people to cry, laugh, dream, love and not give up on hope for a brighter day.

God created us black human beings for His pleasure.

We black human beings had to go through trials and tribulations that our black ancestors went through to make life better for us black human beings today.

God is pleased with us black human beings all around the world, for we are countless like the stars in the universe for God to marvel at us every day.

We black human beings are destined to live in this world with other races of people who God commands us black human beings to love every day, regardless of them looking so different from us.

We black human beings are like the very huge iceberg that sunk the Titanic ship.

Our ancestors broke through the Titanic ships of slavery for us black human beings to be in our rescue boats of democracy today.

God is for us and not against us black human beings to break through the past to heal in the present and to spearhead many good things for us black human beings in the future to come.

We black human beings are like a hot iron to iron out the wrinkles of stereotyping that made many innocent black human beings victims of violence and death, especially in this nation.

We black human beings' humbled and determined ancestors climbed high mountains of hatred so us black people can be where we are all at today in this prosperous land.

We were carried on the backs of our black ancestors who plowed with a mule in the hot sun to plant crops, picked cotton under the hot sun in the fields and worked hard in factories.

Our black ancestors' hard work was technology in their day to help make this nation great today.

We black human beings are so blessed to live in this world with Christian people of every race that have helped us black human beings to know that we are not alone and can hold up the flag of peace over our heads.

Many white Christian people joined in our march for justice and equality.

We black human beings can truly thank God for good people of every race.

Those good people cheered for us black human beings to make it this far in life, and they help us celebrate our victories over the past heartlessness and misfortune.

We black human beings who are saved in Jesus Christ will be made like the angels when we go to heaven when Jesus comes back again.

Nature Knows Our Black Struggles

The sun knows our black struggles and shines down on black lives day after day.

Black love is always eye-catching to Nature that loves to give us black people peace of mind.

The sunlight will radiate it's light all around our black presence, with loyalty to us.

The sun knows our black struggles and rises and sets on our black lives that also matter.

Nature knew the struggles of our black ancestors during the four hundred years of slavery.

The mysterious full white moonlight knows our black struggles and glows so mysteriously down on our black uniqueness.

The full white moonlight will glow its mystic rays all around on our black courage to help us face up to biased people who hate us because of the color of our skin.

The full white moonlight glowed its beautiful light all around on our black ancestors, encouraging them to be bold enough to travel through the night on their way to the north with the moon's light illuminating their path.

All the stars know our black struggles and sparkle down on black dreams as they smile at us with hope.

The stars sparkled down on our black ancestors to let them know that they were embarking on a better day when they would be free.

God created nature to gladly accept us black people, regardless of the sinful nature of human beings.

Nature shows no prejudice against us black people day after day.

Nature shows no partiality against us black people day after day.

The rainbows arch over our black struggles with beautiful colors to remind us that black women are beautiful in every skin complexion.

The beautiful rainbow is God's promise to us black people that He will not destroy this world by water, ever again.

The air knows our black struggles and doesn't discriminate against us, letting us breathe it in and out of our nostrils day after day and night after night.

The air didn't discriminate against our ancestors while many of them made their escape from the South to the North.

The raindrops know our black struggles and fall down on us black people who live in an opinionated land where we are judged by the color of our skin.

The pure white snowflakes know our black struggles and fall down on us black people whose perseverance in this world is pure like the white snowflakes.

Our ancestors didn't do anything so wrong to be put in captivity and sent into slavery.

They were pure like the white snowflakes in their innocence.

God's motives are pure to let us black people exist from the beginning to the end of this world.

The puffy white clouds know our black struggles and puff up with loving and obeying the Lord.

The beautiful green grass knows our black struggles and lets us black people walk on it with dignity every day.

There is a green light of indignity shining over the brown grass of injustice, inequality, and prejudice towards us black people.

The beautiful tall trees know our black struggles and give us their shade and good things to look forward to.

The beautiful trees never wanted to use their limbs to hang any of our black ancestors.

The trees are very sorrowful and truly regret the hangings of the many black men, but there was no remorse in the hearts of many haters of us black people.

The mountains know our black struggles and give us mountaintop experiences of achieving our civil rights goals.

Martin Luther King Jr. saw the mountaintop of a much better life for us black people today.

The ocean waters know our black struggles and refused to swallow down all of our black ancestors in their great depths.

The ocean waters brought many of our ancestors safely over to a land of lies and deceptions that they encountered when they crossed over the ocean waters in ships of captivity.

The ocean waters have marveled at our black ancestors' boldness in accepting a new life of uncertainty in a new land that they would make great by their sweat, hard work, and tears of hope for better days to come to them.

Nature wrote our ancestors' names down in its book for the angels and for you and me to read and know that God was for our black ancestors and not against them.

The early morning fog knew our black struggles and kept many of our ancestors from being captured and sent back to their brutal slave masters.

The dense fog was the camouflage for our ancestors to escape with some peace of mind.

The deep forest sang some songs of victory to our black ancestors, who had to keep their voices down in the deep woods so that no adversary would hear their joy of one day being free.

The sacred ponds know our black struggles, and the ponds gave many of our ancestors some peace as they rested their tired bodies by the sacred waters.

The sacred ponds ministered to their souls about God's amazing love for them.

Nature knows our black struggles every day that nature gives us black people its complete trust, knowing that we will reach our full potential and make this world a better place to live in.

Nature is a gift to us from God, who hung the full white moonlight in the midnight with tears of joy for us black people to prosper in America.

Many of our black ancestors prayed to our Lord and Savior Jesus Christ under the full white moonlight that glowed its bright deliverance upon them.

They prayed in the early morning sunlight and knew that they would rise like the sun in their dreams of being free.

They prayed under the sunset and knew that their descendants would one day rise like the sun and get a good education in this nation.

Our black ancestors prayed to the Lord under all the stars sparkling in the night, and they knew that the stars of time would hug and kiss their visions of freedom from the oppression of slavery.

God used nature to reveal to our ancestors a much better life for generations of their descendants.

Today we know that our black ancestors' hopes, visions, and dreams were not in vain.

The Lord has brought us black people a mighty long way from then to today.

Our black presence has been here for thousands of years.

The Lord has brought us black people so very far and we still have far to go, which even nature would admit.

Nature is also a witness to the police brutality and killing of many young black men who don't get any justice because of haters hating on them every day.

Nature can only stand by and watch all of the injustice crushing down on us black people, but God is still on His holy throne getting justice to our black people who nature loves to be a good friend to every day.

Nature loves us black people, just like nature loves every other race of people.

Nature has never defamed our black existence here in this world where our haters have defamed our black existence and will be held accountable to God on Judgment Day.

The beautiful flowers know our black struggles.

The beautiful flowers comforted many of our black ancestors who took some time out to smell the red roses meaning them good and well on their long journey to the north side of this nation.

The beautiful flowers rescued our ancestors from a lot of mental suffering when they worried about getting caught and taken back to their slave masters who they ran away from for very good reasons.

The beautiful flowers were on their pathway to a beautiful recovery from their adversary's thorns and the dried up weeds of their prejudice and hatred.

Nature knows our black struggles and reminds us that our sinful nature is not to blame for our haters to hate on us.

Their sins of prejudice and hatred are not our sins.

They can't blame us black people for their wrong doings.

God will hold prejudiced people accountable for their sins of hatred that even nature won't accept, for if it did it would lose all of its beauty and glory from God.

The universe knows our black struggles and understands that we black people are victimized by racism every day.

The universe is embarrassed to put up with a world filled with biased people who surely are not representing God who is love and loves everybody no matter the color of their skin.

What Have We Black People Done to You White People?

What have we black people done to you white people?

Many of us black people are peaceful people.

Many of us black people show some love to you white people.

Many of us black people try our best to get along with you white people.

Many of us black people do not judge you white people.

Many of us black people like you white people.

Many of us black people admire you white people.

Many of us black people will never harm you white people.

Many of us black people like our own black people.

You white people don't have to be afraid of every black man.

What have we black people done to you white people to make many of you judge us like many of you do?

What have we black people done to you white people to make many of you hate us like many of you do?

Many of us black people would like to have some good white friends.

Many of us black people don't hold any grudges against you white people, regardless of your many white ancestors who put our black ancestors into slavery.

Many of us black people like the way you white people carry yourselves.

Many of us black people like the way you white people look.

Many of us black people like the way other black people carry themselves.

Many of us black people like the way we black people look.

What have we black people done to you white people to make many of you so prejudiced against us as many of you are?

Many of us black people are good to you white people.

Many of us black people will not do evil things to you white people.

Us good black people don't feel good about bad black people who make all of us black people look bad.

Many of us black people don't have anything against you white people.

Many of us black people try our best to get along with you white people.

Many of us black people do not envy you white people.

Many of us black people don't think badly about you white people.

What have we black people done to you white people to make many of you look down on us like many of you do?

Many of us black people learn a lot of good things from you white people.

Many of us black people also learn a lot of good things from our own black people.

Many of us black people know that there are a lot of good white people.

Many of us black people appreciate good white people.

Many of us black people know that many white people are brilliant.

Many of us black people know that many of our black people are also brilliant.

Many of us black people do not hate white people.

Many of us black people are honest with white people.

What have we black people done to you white people to make many of you treat us so unfairly as many of you do?

Many of us black people will treat you white people fairly.

Many of us black people will treat you white people right.

Many of us black people will treat our own black people right.

Many of us black people will put up with you white people's bad ways.

Many of us black people will put up with our own black people's bad ways.

Many of us black people will not put you white people down.

Many of us black people will not put our own black people down.

What have we black people done to you white people to make many of you oppress us the way many of you do?

Many of us black people will not plot anything against you white people.

Many of us black people will not plot anything against our own black people.

Many of us black people will listen to good advice from you white people.

Many of us black people will listen to good advice from our own black people.

Many of us black people will not give white people a hard time.

Many of us black people will not give our own black people a hard time.

What have we black people done to you white people that makes you disrespect us like many of you do?

Many of us black people do not disrespect you white people.

Many of us black people do not disrespect our own black people.

Many of us black people do trust many of you white people.

Many of us black people do trust many of our own black people.

Many of us black people's hearts are touched by many of you white people.

Many of us black people's hearts are touched by many of our own black people.

Many of us black people do not break under the pressure of you white people.

Many of us black people do not break under the pressure of our own black people.

What have we black people done to you white people that makes many of you want to kill us like many of you do?

Many of us black people will not joke about you white people.

Many of us black people do not joke about our own black people.

Many of us black people believe in Jesus Christ, just like many of you white people do.

Many of us black people are saved in Jesus Christ, just like many of you white people are.

Many of us black people will go to heaven, just like many of you white people who will go to heaven.

What have we black people done to you white people that makes many of you want to talk bad about us and go out of your way to not get to know us?

Many of us black people want to get to know you white people, especially you good white people.

Many of us black people admire the talents and skills that you white people have.

Many of us black people admire the talents and skills our own black people have.

Many of us black people love everybody, regardless of their race, creed or culture.

Many of us black people are peaceful and humble people.

Many of us black people are respectful people.

Many of us black people are strong and joyful people.

Many of us black people will accept you white people for who you are.

Many of us black people know that many of your own white people don't treat you right all of the time.

Many of us black people will stand up for what is right with you white people.

Many of us black people will stand up for what is right with own black people.

What have we black people done to you white people that makes many of you want to segregate yourselves away from us black people?

Many of us black people will look up to many of you white people.

Many of us black people will look up to many of our own black people.

Many of us black people will risk our lives to save you white people.

Many of us black people will risk our lives to save our own black people.

Many of us black people appreciate every race, creed and culture of people.

Many of us black people see beauty in every race, creed and culture of people.

Many of us black people know that God is in every race, creed and culture of people.

What have we black people done to you white people that makes many of you do not want to respect us black people?

Will Not Stop

Stereotyping will not stop many black people from winning Oscars and Emmys and Grammy Awards.

Prejudice will not stop many black people from staying in this nation.

Poverty will not stop many black people from prospering.

Oppression will not stop many black people from getting an education.

Injustice will not stop many black people from loving their neighbors.

Police brutality will not stop many black people from being encouraged.

Mass shootings will not stop many black people from being good.

White privilege will not stop many black people from being determined to defend their human rights.

Discrimination will not stop many black people from chasing after their dreams.

Being dark skinned will not stop many black people from getting rich.

Having nappy hair will not stop many black women from looking beautiful.

Getting laid off from a job will not stop many black people from looking for another job.

Inequality will not stop many black people from respecting everybody.

Having a learning disability will not stop many black people from using their common sense.

No one could stop God from creating black people to live in this world.

No one could stop God from giving many black people some genius, brilliance and intelligence.

No one could stop God from allowing black people to populate this world.

No one could stop God from loving us black people.

No one could stop God from blessing many of us black people.

No one could stop God from sending His only begotten Son to this world to also save us black people from being lost in sin.

Sickness will not stop many black people from working.

Being homeless will not stop many black people from losing hope.

Being in prison will not stop many black people from being sane.

Being single will not stop many black people from finding their soulmate.

Not having a car will not stop many black people from getting to where they want to go.

Being blind will not stop many black people from being successful.

Being deaf will not stop many black people from having a career.

Being paralyzed will not stop many black people from being spiritually, mentally and emotionally strong.

No one could stop God from giving us black people all that we need to survive in this world.

No one could stop God from bringing us black people this far to see this day.

No one could stop God from numbering us black people like the countless stars in the universe.

No one could stop God from allowing many black people to marry white people.

No one could stop God from allowing many black people to buy a new house.

No one could stop God from giving different skin complexions to black people.

No one could stop God from showing His mercy to us black people.

No one could stop God from respecting all of us black people.

Showing favoritism will not disturb many black people.

Misfortunes will not break the hearts of many black people.

Greatness will not go to the heads of many black people.

Trouble will not always last for many black people.

Crabs pulling one another down in a barrel will not always pull down many black people.

No one could stop God from prospering many black people.

No one could stop God from being happy about creating us black people.

No one could stop God from forgiving us black people for our sins.

No one could stop God from building a heavenly mansion for many of us black people.

No one could stop God from giving this world His only begotten Son to save even one sinner as if there was only one black man or black woman being a sinner in this world out of nothing but perfect white people living among one black sinner.

Black is Right for Me

Black is right for me to love the color of my skin, even if everyone else hates the color of my skin.

Black is right for me to believe that I am somebody who can make this world a better place to live in, regardless of being stereotyped.

Black is right for me to hope for a better tomorrow in my life, no matter what I go through today.

Black is right for me to accept who I am being a Christian black man, regardless of the prejudices that surround me day after day.

Black is right for me to enjoy holding onto and never letting go of my Black fulfillment.

Black is right for me to cherish that I am Black with a heart to respect everybody.

Black is right for me to learn from my mistakes and live a life of doing what is right.

Black is right for me to not judge anybody who God will judge.

Black is right for me to tell the truth from my heart to all the world.

Black is right for me to not want to change from being Black because God colored the night black in the black universe with His crayons.

Black is right for me to not bleach my skin to look different from what God has given me.

Black is right for me to be proud of every day, regardless of racism.

Black is right for me to get a good night's sleep and wake up well rested to start a new day being Black.

Black is right for me to believe in Jesus Christ, who shows no respect of persons and loves me and wants to save my soul.

Black is right for me to have no excuse not to give God my best efforts in this life.

Black is right for me to give this world my testimonies about what the Lord brought me through in my life.

Black is right for me to humble myself before the Lord, who doesn't care whether I am Black, white, brown, red or yellow to confess my sins and repent of my sins onto Him.

Black is right for me to give God all the glory and praise that He deserves beyond my blackness.

Black is right for me to carry on my Black ancestor's dreams to make sure they do not fade away in this world of uncertain days.

Black is right for me to never give up on my Lord and Savior Jesus Christ, who created me to be Black and who no one can degrade and get God's approval.

Black is right for me to go to heaven when Jesus Christ comes back again on the clouds of glory for the angels to take me up in and see no color barriers.

Black is right for me to be a blessing to all of my spiritual brothers and sisters, no matter what the color of their skin.

Black is right for me to have no age limit to make achievements in my life.

Black is right for me to choose to make good choices in my life.

Black is right for me to use my common sense that God gave to me.

Black is right for me to know my limits and not overdo things.

Black is right for me to trust my blackness and treat everybody right.

Black is right for me to be in control of myself, even if trouble comes my way.

Black is right for me to not hide my blackness from this world that I don't owe my life to because I owe my life to God.

Black is right for me to never deny that I am Black and not cheat my way through life.

Black is right for me to live my life unto the Lord Jesus Christ, who will never discriminate when giving His love, mercy and grace to me.

Black is right for me to love even my enemies, who can kill my body but not my spirit.

Black is right for me to pray to the Lord with my broken prayers that the Holy Spirit has to fix and make right before God.

Black is right for me to love my neighbors and to love myself for being Black.

Black is right for me to reach up high in life that I will bring myself down from if I know to do right by the Lord and don't do it.

Black is right for me, even if Black is not right for anyone else, as if I am the only one who is Black.

Black is right for me to believe that the color of my skin is the right complexion for me to own it every day.

Black is right for me to lay down and close my eyes into the black, dark unconsciousness that I trust to not harm me in my deep sleep.

Black is right for me to dream away in the black dark and wake up in the consciousness of my blackness.

Black is right for me to honor its presence upon my body that I can joyfully live in every day that my blackness is right for me to live in this world of colorful people of every race.

God created the color of white, the color of black, the color of brown and the color of red and the color of yellow to paint this world and beautify His creation of the human race.

Like The

Like the fresh air we breathe in an out of our nostrils, we black people are breathing the fresh air of our talents in and out of the nostrils of this world.

Like the sun that rises, we black people rise our presence in the workforce.

Like the full, white moonlight that glows so mystical all night long, we black people glow our love so mystical over other races of people to enter into interracial marriages with us black people.

Like the stars that sparkle, we black people sparkle our dreams in this world.

Like the great blue sky that hovers over this world, we black people hover over not giving up our hopes in this world.

Like the high mountain cliffs, we black people are the cliffs of our determination and hard work so we black people can have so much freedom today.

Like the rolling hills, we black people are the rolling hills of democracy to roll our voices on Capitol Hill.

Like the trees that have bird nests in them, we black people are the trees of accepting other races of people to build their nests of ideas in our black lives.

Like the green grass that covers the ground, we black people are the green grass of fearing the Lord even when we black people do bad things and know that we black people are guilty before God on His holy ground.

Like the river that flows, we black people have flowed into the river of integration, especially in many churches.

Like the ocean waves splashing against the rocks on the seashores, we black people are the ocean waves of not accepting inequality for us black people to splash against the rocks of injustice on the seashores of prejudiced people.

Like the birds that fly across the sky, we black people fly our black lives across the sky of white supremacy that loves to shoot us black people down from their sky of hatred like it's a sport.

Like the wind that blows in different directions, we black Christian people blow our faith in Jesus Christ in every direction all around the world to know that Jesus also loves to use us black Christian people to blow His love and redemption in people's hearts all around the world.

I am a Christian Black Man

I am a Christian Black man with a dream to bless this troubled nation because of God's love for me.

I am a Christian Black man to I face up to myself first to be real with God.

This world will stress out my existence from day to day.

I can only be me and love or hate myself in the presence of opinionated people who don't know me.

I am a Christian Black man who is not here by accident.

God came up with a good idea to create me like He wanted to.

God didn't make a mistake when the devil made a mistake to judge me and hate me who can choose to love God and my neighbors.

The devil is my true enemy.

He knows that God didn't create me to be an empty shell.

The sand can run out of an hourglass.

A star can fall from the sky.

A shadow can disappear.

I am a Christian Black man who God created for eternity beyond the things that are temporary and can end.

I am a Christian Black man who can love everybody, even though many people hate me for being Black.

I am somebody to God, even if nobody else cares.

I am a human being who God created in His image, and I think, reason and live to worship Him.

I am not an animal that can't think and can't reason things out.

When you see me, you can see that I am a human being like you.

You may want to hate me or kill be for no good reason, even though you may believe you have a good reason.

I am a Christian Black man all day and all night long.

My color won't change for you, even if you have a problem with the color of my skin.

Jesus Christ, my Lord and Savior, died on the cross for my sins too.

He didn't leave me out of His salvation because I am black.

When you see me in heaven, don't be shocked.

Heaven is for the Christian black man too.

I love who I am, and I am black, not Asian, Jewish white or Arab, or any other race.

If you have a problem with me being black, then you need to talk to God about it.

I am a Christian Black man who was born to be black.

Life welcomes me into this world because I was meant to be here to do God's will.

Being black is a problem for anyone who doesn't love God.

God says that if you say you love Him who you don't see but hate your brother who you do see, then you are a liar.

I am your black brother who you do see.

I am a Christian Black man existing to live in a sinful world where the devil is my real, true enemy who tries to pollute my soul so it will be lost.

I am a Christian Black man walking through the wilderness of the uncertain that loves to try to make me think living my life is in vain.

God has made my life worth living and I strive to be like the sound of gospel songs.

My blackness will follow me wherever I go.

It will attract some attention, and some will accept me for being black.

I am a Christian Black man who is a controversial subject to the devil.

He knows that if I love Jesus Christ, he lost his victory over me.

I am a Christian Black man who is no island sitting all alone in the ocean.

God will stand me up in the middle of his angels every day.

God created me to be a black man who he approves of in this world and in the new world to come one day.

Could it be profound to God to create a black man to be different from all other men of different races?

God is matchless, so who can question God for creating a black man like me?

I am a Christian Black man who is tossed on every side of the world by people stereotyping me like poisonous fumes coming out of an exhaust pipe.

My Lord and Savior Jesus Christ has renewed my life for me to be a Christian Black man.

His love is just like clean air to breathe in and out day after day.

Ignorance will conspire against me and injustice will gladly accuse me of not being a Christian black man day after day in a world that shows favoritism to the white privileged, even though many white people don't believe it.

I am a Christian Black man who God favors to live in this world and claim my existence.

I am a Christian Black man who the sun will shine down on with respect.

The full white moon will glow down on me with respect.

The rainbow will arch up high over me with respect.

The rain and snow will fall down on me with respect.

Nature will surround me with respect.

Nature will treat me as no less of a man than any other man of any race, creed or culture of men.

I am a Christian Black man for others to see and greatly accept when Jesus comes back again.

www.ingramcontent.com/pod-product-compliance
Lightning Source LLC
Chambersburg PA
CBHW070940120626
46546CB00004B/1501